THINKING
VS
THOUGHT

TAPPING INTO UNIVERSAL WISDOM

WRITTEN BY
MIKE JENSEN

Copyright © 2024 by Mike Jensen

All rights reserved.

Published and Distributed in Canada by Live Life Happy Publishing.
www.livelifehappypublishing.com

All rights reserved. No part of this book may be reproduced by any mechanical, photographic, or electronic process, or in the form of a phonograph recording: Nor may it be stored in a retrieval system, transmitted, or otherwise be copied for public or private use- other than for "fair use" as brief quotations embodied in articles and reviews without prior written permission of the publisher. If you use any of the information in this book for yourself, which is your constitutional right, the author and the publisher assumes no responsibility for your actions.

Library of Congress Cataloging-in-Publication Data

Mike Jensen

Thinking Vs Thought

Medical Books > Psychology > Cognitive > Self-Help > Personal Transformation > Politics & Social Sciences > Philosophy > Consciousness & Thought

ISBN: 978-1-998724-10-9 E-Book

ISBN: 978-1-998724-09-3 Paperback

Cover Design: Mike Jensen

Live Life Happy Publishing

PUBLISHER'S NOTE & AUTHOR DISCLAIMER

This publication is designed to provide accurate and authoritative information concerning the subject matter covered. It is sold to understand that the publisher and author are not engaging in or rendering any psychological, medical or other professional services. If expert assistance or counselling is needed, seek the services of a competent medical professional. For immediate support call your local crisis line. The following book could contain actual events and experiences that the author has encountered in their life. However, some names and specific locations have been changed or omitted to protect the privacy and confidentiality of the individuals involved. The changes do not alter the story's integrity or its messages.

TABLE OF CONTENT

Introduction 5

Chapter 1: The Mind and Body A Dynamic Partnership 7

Chapter 2: The Unconscious Mind Efficiency in Action 13

Chapter 3: Universe Knowledge and Thought 21

Chapter 4: Steps to Enhance Your Performance 29

Chapter 5: Understanding "Universe Knowledge" 37

Chapter 6: How Universe Knowledge
Defeats Current Challenges 47

Chapter 7: Applying Universe Knowledge
in Everyday Life 57

Chapter 8: The Synergy of Thinking and Thought 67

Chapter 9: Balancing Thinking and Thought 75

Chapter 10: The Role of Presence in Unlocking
Universe Knowledge 85

Chapter 11: Trusting the Flow of Universe Knowledge 95

Chapter 12: The Role of Action in 105

Chapter 13: Living in Alignment with
Universe Knowledge 115

Chapter 14: The Ongoing Journey
of Universe Knowledge 125

INTRODUCTION

Tapping Into Universal Knowledge

"Universe Knowledge quickly defeats whatever now defeats you."

— *Vernon Howard*

Imagine a world where your toughest challenges—uncertainty, stress, or self-doubt—are dissolved by tapping into a well of infinite insight. Picture yourself navigating life with a clear, intuitive compass, making decisions that feel both effortless and profound. This is the power of universal knowledge—a boundless reservoir of wisdom available to everyone who seeks it.

This book explores the delicate interplay between "thinking" and "thought", two cognitive processes that shape every decision, action, and outcome in our lives. Thinking is the structured, logical process of analyzing and solving problems; thought is the spontaneous, intuitive spark that often leads to breakthroughs. When balanced, these forces unlock unparalleled creativity, clarity, and purpose.

But how do you access and harness this universal knowledge? The journey begins by understanding the tools already within you—your mind and body—and learning how to balance deliberate thought with intuitive insight. Together, these concepts form the foundation of a life filled with meaningful decisions, enhanced performance, and an extraordinary connection to the world around you.

Through engaging examples, reflective exercises, and actionable strategies, this book will guide you on a journey to:

- Tap into your intuition while mastering logical thinking.
- Overcome challenges using universal principles.
- Cultivate a balanced mind that fosters creativity, resilience, and growth.

By the end of this book, you'll not only understand the difference between thinking and thought but also know how to harmonize them in your daily life to achieve lasting fulfillment.

CHAPTER 1

THE MIND AND BODY A DYNAMIC PARTNERSHIP

Think of the most advanced robot you've ever seen. Imagine its sleek hardware performing intricate movements with ease, all controlled by a cutting-edge computer system. Now, replace the robot with your body and the computer with your mind. Together, they form a seamless partnership, enabling you to navigate life with remarkable precision.

But like any partnership, the relationship between your mind and body depends on balance, understanding, and care.

Mind as the Controller

Your mind is the command center, constantly processing sensory inputs, making decisions, and directing your body's actions. For instance, when you touch a hot stove, your brain rapidly processes the signal and tells your hand to pull away. This partnership is what allows you to respond to the world around you.

However, the mind isn't just logical. It's also emotional, shaping your actions through feelings like fear, joy, or determination. Consider the nervous energy before a big presentation—it sharpens your focus but can also paralyze you if unchecked. This dual role of the mind highlights the need for emotional awareness to maintain harmony.

Body as the Mechanism

Your body, like the hardware of a robot, carries out tasks with precision. Whether it's typing, running, or creating art, your body's efficiency depends on how well you maintain it. For example, proper nutrition fuels your "hardware," while sleep restores your system.

But the body isn't just a machine—it's deeply intuitive. Ever had a "gut feeling"? That's your body communicating through subtle signals. Learning to listen to these cues enhances the synergy between your mind and body.

The Power of Habits

When mind and body work together, they create habits that simplify life. Think of learning to drive a car. At first, every action—turning the wheel, pressing the gas—requires deliberate thought. Over time, these actions become second nature, handled by your subconscious mind.

This phenomenon, known as muscle memory, extends beyond physical tasks. It influences behaviors, emotions, and thought patterns. By cultivating positive habits, you train your mind and body to operate in harmony, unlocking higher efficiency and ease.

Modern Challenges to Mind-Body Balance

In today's fast-paced world, distractions often sever the connection between mind and body. Constant notifications, stress, and multitasking overwhelm the mind, leaving little room for intuitive thought. To restore balance, intentional practices like mindfulness and movement are essential.

············ **Key Insights** ············

1. Understand the Partnership: Your mind is the controller, and your body is the mechanism. Together, they shape your actions and reactions.

CHAPTER ONE: THE MIND AND BODY A DYNAMIC PARTNERSHIP

2. Cultivate Positive Habits: Repeated actions strengthen the mind-body connection, improving efficiency and reducing mental strain.

3. Listen to Intuition: Your body communicates through sensations and emotions—tune into these signals for better decision-making.

4. Embrace Mindfulness: Practices like meditation can reestablish the connection between mind and body, helping you stay present.

Reflection Questions

1. Can you recall a moment when your mind and body worked seamlessly, like reacting quickly in a high-pressure situation? What made it possible?

2. What habits could you develop to strengthen your mind-body connection?

3. How does stress or overthinking disrupt your natural instincts, and what steps could you take to restore balance?

CHAPTER 2

THE UNCONSCIOUS MIND EFFICIENCY IN ACTION

Imagine standing at a busy intersection. Without conscious effort, your senses process the flashing walk signal, the sound of approaching cars, and the feel of the pavement beneath your feet. You begin walking at the right moment, seamlessly navigating the flow of traffic. This automatic precision isn't magic—it's the power of your unconscious mind at work

CHAPTER TWO: THE UNCONSCIOUS MIND EFFICIENCY IN ACTION

Understanding the Unconscious Mind

The unconscious mind operates behind the scenes, handling countless processes that allow us to function efficiently. It governs everything from breathing and digestion to deeply ingrained habits and split-second reactions. Unlike conscious thought, which is deliberate and slow, the unconscious mind is fast, automatic, and incredibly efficient.

Consider an athlete making a game-winning play. A soccer player intercepts a pass, pivots, and scores—all in a matter of seconds. Their conscious mind isn't giving step-by-step instructions. Instead, years of training have programmed their unconscious mind to react instinctively, allowing them to perform with precision and speed.

The Role of Repetition and Practice

The unconscious mind learns through repetition. Each time you repeat a task, you strengthen the neural pathways associated with that activity, making it easier and faster to perform. This process is why practice is so essential in mastering any skill.

For example, when you first learned to type, each keystroke required deliberate effort. Over time, your unconscious mind took over, enabling you to type effortlessly while thinking about other things. This phenomenon, often called "muscle memory," applies to mental tasks as well, such as solving familiar problems or recalling information quickly.

Key Insight: The more consistently you practice a skill or habit, the more your unconscious mind optimizes and automates the process.

The Limits of the Unconscious Mind

While the unconscious mind is efficient, it's not infallible. It relies on patterns, which can be both beneficial and harmful. For instance, habits like exercising regularly are examples of positive programming. Conversely, negative habits—like procrastination or reacting defensively—are also the result of unconscious conditioning.

To reprogram unhelpful patterns, you must bring them into conscious awareness. Once identified, intentional practice can overwrite these patterns with healthier alternatives.

Example: *A person who unconsciously avoids confrontation might recognize this tendency during reflection. By consciously practicing assertiveness in small, manageable steps, they can retrain their unconscious reactions over time.*

Intuition: The Voice of the Unconscious Mind

The unconscious mind often communicates through intuition—a sudden feeling, insight, or "gut instinct." Intuition arises when the brain processes vast amounts of information subconsciously, leading to quick judgments or solutions.

For example, a seasoned teacher might sense that a student is struggling emotionally before any outward signs are apparent. Their intuition is informed by years of observing subtle cues like body language or tone of voice.

However, intuition is not always accurate. It can be influenced by biases or incomplete information. The key is to balance intuitive insights with analytical thinking, ensuring your decisions are both informed and instinctive.

Harnessing the Power of the Unconscious Mind

To make the most of your unconscious mind, focus on three areas:

1. **Repetition and Visualization:** Practice skills consistently and use visualization to mentally rehearse desired outcomes. Athletes, for example, often imagine themselves executing perfect performances to train their brains.

2. **Mindfulness:** Cultivate awareness of unconscious habits and thought patterns. Practices like meditation help you notice automatic responses, creating opportunities to reshape them.

3. **Trust Your Intuition (Within Reason):** While intuition can guide you, balance it with logical analysis. If your gut instinct feels off, take a step back and evaluate the situation objectively.

Key Insights

1. **Efficiency Through Automation:** The unconscious mind handles repetitive tasks, freeing your conscious mind for more complex decisions.

2. **Practice Makes Permanent:** Habits and skills become automated through consistent repetition, forming neural pathways that support efficiency.

3. **The Power of Intuition:** Intuition is a valuable tool for quick decision-making but must be balanced with conscious reasoning.

4. **Reprogramming Habits:** Identifying and reshaping unhelpful unconscious patterns requires mindfulness and deliberate effort.

Reflection Questions

1. Think of a time when your unconscious mind helped you perform a task effortlessly, like driving or solving a problem quickly. How did it feel?

2. Are there any habits or automatic reactions you'd like to change? How could mindfulness and practice help reprogram them?

CHAPTER TWO: THE UNCONSCIOUS MIND EFFICIENCY IN ACTION

3. Can you recall a moment when your intuition guided you correctly—or led you astray? What can you learn from that experience?

4. How could you use visualization to strengthen a skill or prepare for a challenge?

CHAPTER 3

UNIVERSE KNOWLEDGE AND THOUGHT

Imagine standing beneath a starry sky, feeling the vastness of the universe above. In that moment, you sense a profound connection to something greater than yourself—a timeless energy that weaves together every star, planet, and living being. This is the essence of universal knowledge—a limitless source of insight that transcends logic, offering clarity, creativity, and purpose.

Accessing this knowledge requires learning to quiet the mind, embrace intuition, and trust in the deeper layers of awareness.

What Is Universe Knowledge?

Universe knowledge refers to an interconnected intelligence that transcends individual thought. It is not bound by logic or conscious effort but instead flows naturally when the mind is still and receptive. This type of insight often manifests as a sudden realization or an intuitive idea that feels profoundly true.

Example: *Consider moments of inspiration described by creative individuals. A composer might suddenly hear a melody in their mind or a scientist might experience a breakthrough idea while taking a walk. These insights often feel as though they come "from nowhere," yet they stem from the deep reservoir of universe knowledge.*

The Connection Between Thought and Universe Knowledge

"Thought" acts as the bridge to this universal intelligence. While "thinking" involves deliberate, logical processes, "thought" is spontaneous and intuitive. It arises when you're relaxed, open, and detached from over analysis.

Comparison:
- Thinking: Problem-solving through conscious effort, step by step.

- Thought: Receiving insights effortlessly, often as flashes of intuition.

When thinking dominates, it can block access to universe knowledge by creating mental noise. For example, overanalyzing a problem might obscure a simple, intuitive solution that emerges when the mind is quiet.

How to Access Universe Knowledge

1. **Relaxation and Stillness:** The first step to accessing universe knowledge is quieting the mind. Practices like meditation, deep breathing, or spending time in nature help calm mental chatter and create space for intuitive thoughts to arise.

Practical Tip: Try this simple exercise:
- Sit in a quiet space.
- Take deep breaths, focusing on the sensation of air entering and leaving your body.
- When your mind begins to wander, gently return your attention to your breath.

Even five minutes of this practice can enhance clarity and open you to deeper insights.

2. **Asking Purposeful Questions:** The universe often responds to clear, intentional questions. When seeking answers, phrase your questions thoughtfully and remain open to unexpected responses.

Example: *If you're uncertain about a career decision, ask yourself, "What step aligns with my purpose?" Then, remain attentive to intuitive nudges, whether they come as a sudden thought, a meaningful dream, or a chance encounter.*

3. **Trust the Process:** Answers from universe knowledge may not arrive immediately or in expected forms. Patience and trust are essential. Recognize that insights often appear when you least expect them—while walking, showering, or engaging in a repetitive task.

Barriers to Universe Knowledge

While this intelligence is always available, certain habits can block access:

- **Overthinking:** Excessive mental effort creates noise that drowns out intuitive insights.

- **Distracted Living:** Constant exposure to technology or stress leaves little room for stillness.

- **Doubt:** Dismissing intuitive thoughts as illogical or irrelevant prevents you from exploring their potential.

Overcoming Barriers:
- Incorporate daily mindfulness practices to reduce mental clutter.

- Limit distractions by setting boundaries around technology use.

- Cultivate curiosity and openness toward intuitive ideas, even if they initially seem unconventional.

Universe Knowledge in Action

This interconnected intelligence is not just theoretical—it has practical applications in creativity, problem-solving, and decision-making.

Example 1: *Creativity: Writers, artists, and inventors often describe moments of inspiration that feel like "downloads" from the universe. For instance, Albert Einstein credited many of his scientific insights to intuitive thought rather than deliberate analysis.*

Example 2: *Problem-Solving: In complex situations, stepping back and allowing space for intuition often leads to elegant solutions. Think of a time when you struggled with a problem, only for the answer to appear after taking a break or sleeping on it.*

Example 3: *Everyday Decisions: Even mundane choices—like choosing a route to work—can benefit from intuitive guidance. For instance, you might instinctively decide to take a different path and later discover you avoided traffic or encountered a meaningful opportunity.*

Strengthening Your Connection to Universe Knowledge

1. **Daily Visualization:** Visualize yourself connected to an infinite stream of light or energy, representing universal intelligence. Imagine this energy flowing into you, bringing clarity and wisdom.

2. **Keep a Journal:** Document intuitive thoughts, dreams, and sudden insights. Over time, patterns may emerge that deepen your understanding of how universe knowledge communicates with you.

3. **Experiment with Intuition:** Practice small experiments to sharpen your intuitive skills. For instance, guess who's calling before picking up the phone or predicting the outcome of a simple event. These exercises build trust in your inner guidance.

Key Insights

1. Universe knowledge is an infinite source of wisdom accessible through thought and intuition.

2. Relaxation and mindfulness are essential for quieting mental chatter and opening the mind to universal insights.

3. Purposeful questions and trust in the process help you receive and interpret intuitive guidance.

4. Overcoming barriers like overthinking and distractions enhances your connection to this deeper intelligence.

Reflection Questions

1. Have you ever experienced a sudden, intuitive insight that felt like it came from beyond your conscious mind? How did you act on it?

2. What steps can you take to quiet your mind and create space for universe knowledge to emerge?

3. How might you use visualization or journaling to strengthen your connection to universal intelligence?

4. Reflect on a challenge you're currently facing. How could you balance thinking and thought to approach it differently?

CHAPTER 4

STEPS TO ENHANCE YOUR PERFORMANCE

Imagine you're preparing for an important event—a job interview, a sports competition, or a creative performance. You've practiced, analyzed every detail, and rehearsed your steps, yet there's something else at play when the moment arrives. The ability to perform at your best often depends on something deeper: trusting the connection between your mind, body, and intuition.

This chapter explores practical steps to improve performance by harmonizing thinking (logical analysis) with thought (intuitive flow). By balancing these elements, you can elevate your capabilities in any area of life.

CHAPTER FOUR: STEPS TO ENHANCE YOUR PERFORMANCE

The Role of Intuition in Performance

When you rely solely on analytical thinking, you may become bogged down by over analysis, second-guessing your decisions. On the other hand, fully trusting intuition without preparation can lead to inconsistency. The key to optimal performance lies in integrating these processes: using thinking to build a solid foundation and thought to execute with fluidity and confidence.

Example: *A musician practices scales and chords (thinking) to build technical proficiency. But during a live performance, they rely on thought to improvise and connect emotionally with their audience. The technical foundation allows intuition to flow freely.*

Step 1: Build Trust in Your Intuition

Developing trust in your intuition starts with small, deliberate actions. Pay attention to gut feelings in low-stakes situations and reflect on their accuracy.

Exercise:
- Before making a simple decision (e.g., choosing a route to work), pause and consider your intuitive choice.

- Act on this instinct and reflect on the outcome. Did it feel right?

Over time, these exercises strengthen your confidence in intuition, making it easier to trust in high-pressure scenarios.

Step 2: Quiet Your Mind

To perform at your best, you need mental clarity. Practices like mindfulness, meditation, or progressive muscle relaxation help reduce distractions and create a calm mental state.

Example: *Athletes often visualize success before competing. A sprinter might mentally rehearse their perfect start, feeling the power in their legs and hearing the sound of the starting gun. This quiet focus primes their mind and body for peak performance.*

Practical Tip:
- Spend 5–10 minutes before any important task practicing deep breathing or visualization. Focus on the desired outcome and let go of unnecessary thoughts.

Step 3: Learn to Switch Between Thinking and Thought

Performance often requires alternating between deliberate thinking and intuitive action. For example, a chef might analyze a recipe while planning a meal but rely on instinct to adjust flavors during cooking.

How to Practice Switching Modes:
1. **Start with structured planning:** Break tasks into steps, create checklists, or gather necessary tools.

2. **Once the groundwork is laid, shift into a state of flow:** Trust your preparation and focus on the experience itself, rather than micromanaging every detail.

Step 4: Practice Under Pressure

Stress can disrupt the balance between thinking and thought, leading to either over analysis or impulsive decisions. To perform well in high-pressure situations, expose yourself to controlled stress during practice.

Example: *A public speaker can practice delivering a speech in front of a small audience to simulate the experience of being on stage. This builds familiarity with the pressure, reducing anxiety when the stakes are higher.*

Exercise:
- Gradually increase the complexity of tasks under time constraints or in challenging environments.

- Reflect on how you respond to pressure and adjust your strategies as needed.

Step 5: Leverage Visualization and Repetition

Visualization trains your brain to anticipate success, while repetition ingrains positive habits into your subconscious. These tools reinforce the connection between your mind and body, ensuring smooth performance.

Visualization Technique:
1. Close your eyes and imagine yourself completing a task flawlessly.

2. Engage all your senses—what does it look, sound, and feel like?

3. Repeat this exercise daily to condition your mind for success.

Repetition Example: *A dancer rehearsing a routine multiple times develops muscle memory, allowing their body to perform effortlessly when the music starts.*

Step 6: Embrace Feedback and Adaptability

Feedback is essential for growth. Whether it comes from mentors, peers, or your own reflections, use it to refine your skills and enhance performance.

Example: *A writer might share a draft with trusted readers and use their insights to improve the final piece. This iterative process blends analytical thinking (editing) with intuitive creativity (spontaneous revisions).*

Adaptability Tip:
- View setbacks as learning opportunities. Ask yourself, "What can I adjust next time to improve?"

CHAPTER FOUR: STEPS TO ENHANCE YOUR PERFORMANCE

Balancing Logic and Instinct

Optimal performance happens when preparation (thinking) and trust in the moment (thought) are in harmony. If you feel stuck in one mode, try the following:

- **Too Much Thinking:** Pause, take a deep breath, and focus on the immediate task instead of overanalyzing.

- **Too Much Instinct:** Step back and review your strategy to ensure you're on track.

Key Insights

1. Trusting your intuition requires practice in low-stakes situations before applying it to more significant challenges.

2. Mindfulness and visualization help reduce distractions and prepare your mind for success.

3. Alternating between thinking and thought allows you to plan carefully while staying adaptable in the moment.

4. Controlled exposure to pressure builds confidence and resilience in high-stakes situations.

5. Feedback and adaptability are critical for continuous improvement.

Reflection Questions

1. Can you think of a time when trusting your intuition led to better performance? How did you build the confidence to rely on it?

2. What mindfulness practices could you adopt to create mental clarity before important tasks?

3. How do you currently balance preparation and adaptability in your daily life? Are there areas where you could improve?

4. Reflect on a recent challenge where feedback helped you grow. How can you seek constructive feedback more regularly?

5. How might visualization and repetition enhance a specific skill or goal you're currently working on?

CHAPTER 5

UNDERSTANDING "UNIVERSE KNOWLEDGE"

Have you ever marveled at the intricate design of nature—a tree's ability to turn sunlight into life, or the way rivers carve landscapes over millennia? These phenomena illustrate universal principles that connect everything in existence. By understanding and aligning with these principles, you gain access to a profound intelligence woven into the fabric of the universe.

In this chapter, we'll explore the layers of universe knowledge—scientific, philosophical, spiritual, and practical—and how integrating these perspectives can help you unlock deeper understanding and purpose in your life

The Four Dimensions of Universe Knowledge

1. Scientific Knowledge: The Blueprint of Reality

Science offers a structured way to understand the physical world through observation, experimentation, and analysis. It reveals the mechanics behind natural phenomena and helps us solve practical problems.

Examples of Universal Scientific Principles:
- **Gravity:** A force that governs motion, from the fall of an apple to the orbit of planets.

- **Ecosystems:** Interdependent networks where each species plays a role in maintaining balance.

- **Energy Conservation:** A fundamental truth that energy cannot be created or destroyed, only transformed.

Application: *Understanding scientific principles helps us navigate the physical world more effectively. For instance, knowing the principles of nutrition and exercise allows us to care for our bodies, while studying physics enables technological advancements.*

2. Philosophical Knowledge: The Search for Meaning

Philosophy examines the deeper questions of life—Who are we? Why are we here? How should we live? It provides tools to reflect on existence, ethics, and the nature of reality.

Core Philosophical Concepts:

•   Metaphysics: Explores what exists beyond the physical, such as the nature of consciousness.

•   Ethics: Guides us in determining right from wrong, shaping our interactions with others.

•   Logic: Enhances critical thinking, helping us evaluate ideas and arguments effectively.

Example: *The Greek philosopher Aristotle believed that everything in the universe has a purpose or "final cause." Applying this idea, you might reflect on your life's purpose, aligning your actions with a deeper sense of fulfillment.*

3. Spiritual Knowledge: Connecting to the Infinite

Spirituality goes beyond intellectual understanding, fostering a connection with something greater than oneself. Whether through religious practices, meditation, or personal reflection, spiritual knowledge nurtures inner peace and a sense of purpose.

Spiritual Principles:
- **Interconnectedness:** Recognizing that all beings are part of a unified whole.

- **Mindfulness:** Cultivating awareness of the present moment to reduce stress and gain clarity.

- **Karma:** Understanding the ripple effect of actions on the world around us.

Application: *Spiritual practices help you tap into universal wisdom and find harmony. For example, mindfulness meditation can calm your mind, allowing intuitive insights to emerge.*

4. Practical Knowledge: Bridging Theory and Action

Practical knowledge translates abstract ideas into tangible actions. It involves skills, problem-solving, and lessons learned from personal experience.

Key Areas of Practical Knowledge:
- **Critical Thinking:** Analyzing situations to make informed decisions.

- **Communication:** Sharing ideas effectively to foster understanding and collaboration.

- **Adaptability:** Learning from setbacks and adjusting to new circumstances.

Example: *Consider a community facing an environmental challenge. Practical knowledge might involve applying scientific data, ethical reasoning, and spiritual values to create a sustainable solution.*

Integrating Universe Knowledge

When combined, these four dimensions create a holistic framework for understanding life.

Illustration:
- Scientific knowledge explains the how (e.g., how ecosystems function).

- Philosophical knowledge asks the why (e.g., why we should preserve nature).

- Spiritual knowledge connects us to the bigger picture (e.g., recognizing our role as stewards of the Earth).

- Practical knowledge empowers us to take action (e.g., implementing conservation strategies).

By weaving these perspectives together, you gain a deeper appreciation for the complexity and unity of the universe.

Applications of Universe Knowledge

1. Decision-Making
When faced with a tough choice, consider all dimensions:

CHAPTER FIVE: UNDERSTANDING "UNIVERSE KNOWLEDGE"

- Use scientific knowledge to evaluate facts.

- Apply philosophical reasoning to align with your values.

- Trust spiritual intuition for clarity.

- Take practical steps to execute your decision effectively.

Example: *Choosing a career might involve researching job prospects (scientific), reflecting on your purpose (philosophical), trusting your instincts (spiritual), and building the necessary skills (practical).*

2. Creativity and Innovation
Many groundbreaking ideas emerge from combining different types of knowledge.

- Scientific research informs artistic mediums, like digital design.

- Philosophical exploration inspires stories and art.

- Spiritual reflection fuels emotional depth in creative works.

- Practical skills bring these ideas to life.

Example: *The invention of renewable energy technologies like solar panels reflects a blend of scientific knowledge, ethical considerations, and a commitment to practical solutions.*

Barriers to Embracing Universe Knowledge

1. **Fragmented Thinking:** Focusing on one dimension while neglecting others leads to imbalance.

2. **Cynicism:** Dismissing philosophical or spiritual insights as irrelevant can limit growth.

3. **Overwhelming Complexity:** Universe knowledge is vast, but breaking it into manageable steps makes it accessible.

Solution: *Approach universal knowledge with curiosity and patience, seeking connections rather than perfection.*

Key Insights

1. Universe knowledge encompasses scientific, philosophical, spiritual, and practical dimensions, each contributing unique perspectives.

2. Integrating these dimensions creates a holistic approach to understanding and solving life's challenges.

3. By reflecting on universal principles, you align your actions with a greater sense of purpose and meaning.

4. Small, consistent steps—like exploring new ideas or practicing mindfulness—deepen your connection to universe knowledge.

Reflection Questions

1. How do scientific principles, like gravity or ecosystems, influence your understanding of the world?

2. Reflect on a philosophical idea (e.g., purpose or ethics) that has shaped your values. How does it guide your decisions?

3. What spiritual practices (e.g., meditation, gratitude) help you feel connected to a larger whole?

4. How can you integrate practical knowledge, such as critical thinking or adaptability, into your daily challenges?

5. Consider the current problem you're facing. How could you apply all four dimensions of universe knowledge to find a solution?

CHAPTER 6

HOW UNIVERSE KNOWLEDGE DEFEATS CURRENT CHALLENGES

Imagine facing a challenge so overwhelming it feels insurmountable—a career setback, a relationship conflict, or even a global crisis. Now, envision approaching that same challenge with a clear sense of purpose, equipped with the wisdom of interconnected principles that help you see beyond the immediate problem. This is the power of universe knowledge: a multidimensional framework that helps you overcome obstacles by uncovering deeper truths and solutions.

In this chapter, we'll explore how applying universe knowledge to life's challenges can offer clarity, creativity, and resilience.

CHAPTER SIX: HOW UNIVERSE KNOWLEDGE DEFEATS CURRENT CHALLENGES

The Transformative Perspective of Universe Knowledge

Challenges often feel daunting because we view them in isolation, focusing only on immediate outcomes. Universe knowledge helps shift this perspective by showing the bigger picture—how problems are interconnected with larger systems and how solutions ripple outward.

Example: *Consider environmental challenges like climate change. At first glance, they seem overwhelming. However, by recognizing the interconnectedness of social, economic, and environmental systems, we can design solutions that address multiple factors, such as renewable energy innovation and sustainable policies.*

Shifting Perspective to Gain Clarity

A core principle of universe knowledge is that challenges are not permanent. By taking a broader view, you can reframe obstacles as opportunities for growth.

Practical Exercise: When faced with a challenge, ask yourself:
1. What is this teaching me? Shift your focus from frustration to learning.

2. How does this fit into a larger context? Consider how this problem connects to broader patterns in your life or the world.

3. What ripple effects could my solution create? Envision the positive impact of resolving the issue.

Example: *A personal conflict might initially feel like a deadlock, but viewing it through the lens of interconnectedness could reveal underlying communication patterns. By addressing these, you not only resolve the immediate issue but also improve future interactions.*

The Power of Systems Thinking

Universe knowledge encourages systems thinking—a method of understanding how components of a problem influence one another. This approach prevents short-term fixes that ignore deeper causes.

Example: *A business struggling with employee retention might initially address surface-level issues like salaries. However, applying systems thinking could reveal deeper factors, such as workplace culture or lack of growth opportunities, leading to a more effective, sustainable solution.*

Actionable Tip: To apply systems thinking:
- Map out all factors contributing to the challenge.

- Identify relationships between these factors.

- Focus on changes that create positive ripple effects.

Applying Scientific Principles to Problem-Solving

1. Observation: Start by identifying what's happening without judgment.

2. Experimentation: Test small changes to see what works.

3. Iteration: Refine your approach based on results.

Example: *A student struggling with time management might begin by observing their daily habits, experimenting with scheduling techniques, and iterating based on what improves productivity.*

Philosophy: Questioning Assumptions

Philosophy encourages critical thinking, helping you challenge assumptions and explore new perspectives.

Questions to Reflect On:
- Are my beliefs about this problem limiting my options?

- Am I focusing on short-term relief rather than long-term growth?

- How would I view this challenge if I were in someone else's position?

Example: *A team leader might assume that conflict arises because team members lack effort. By questioning this assumption, they might discover that unclear communication or differing work styles are the root causes.*

Spiritual Practices for Emotional Resilience

Spiritual knowledge enhances your ability to stay calm and centered during challenges, helping you make thoughtful decisions. Practices like mindfulness, gratitude, and meditation cultivate emotional resilience by grounding you in the present moment.

Practical Exercise:
- Mindful Breathing: Take 5 minutes to focus solely on your breath, letting go of distractions.

- Gratitude Journaling: Write down three things you're grateful for each day to shift focus from stress to appreciation.

- Visualization: Imagine yourself successfully overcoming the challenge and the positive outcomes that will follow.

Personal Connection and Growth

Every challenge holds the potential for personal growth. Universe knowledge helps you view difficulties as stepping stones to greater understanding and capability.

CHAPTER SIX: HOW UNIVERSE KNOWLEDGE DEFEATS CURRENT CHALLENGES

Example: *A failed project might initially feel like a setback. However, by reflecting on what went wrong and integrating those lessons, you gain skills and insights that lead to future success.*

Key Mindset Shift: Rather than asking, "Why is this happening to me?" ask, "What is this preparing me for?"

Collaboration: Harnessing Collective Wisdom

Some challenges are too complex to solve alone. Collaboration allows you to pool diverse perspectives, leveraging the unique strengths and experiences of others.

Example: *During a community crisis, a team of healthcare workers, educators, and social leaders might collaborate to address not just the immediate needs but also the underlying causes.*

Collaboration Tip:
- Approach collaboration with humility and curiosity.

- Focus on shared goals rather than individual agendas.

- Celebrate small wins along the way to maintain the right type of motivation.

The Role of Continuous Learning

Universe knowledge emphasizes lifelong learning as a way to navigate challenges effectively. Staying curious and open to new ideas equips you with fresh tools and perspectives for problem-solving.

Actionable Steps:
1. **Expand Your Knowledge Base:** Read books, attend workshops, or take courses related to the challenge.

2. **Embrace Feedback:** Seek constructive criticism to refine your approach.

3. **Experiment Boldly:** Try new strategies, even if they feel uncomfortable at first.

Key Insights

1. Shifting perspective helps reframe challenges as opportunities for growth and connection.

2. Systems thinking reveals the interconnected causes of problems, enabling sustainable solutions.

3. Spiritual practices like mindfulness and gratitude foster emotional resilience during difficult times.

4. Collaboration amplifies your ability to address complex issues by leveraging collective wisdom.

5. Lifelong learning ensures you're continually adapting and evolving in response to challenges.

Reflection Questions

1. Can you recall a challenge that felt insurmountable at first but became manageable after shifting your perspective? What changed?

2. How could you apply systems thinking to a current problem in your life or work?

3. Which spiritual practices—mindfulness, gratitude, or visualization—might help you stay centered during tough times?

4. Reflect on a time when collaboration helped you solve a complex issue. How did diverse perspectives shape the solution?

5. What new skills or knowledge could you explore to better address a current challenge?

CHAPTER 7

APPLYING UNIVERSE KNOWLEDGE IN EVERYDAY LIFE

THINKING VS THOUGHT

Imagine starting your day with clarity, confidence, and a sense of purpose, knowing you have access to a limitless reservoir of wisdom to guide your decisions. From choosing what to prioritize at work to resolving personal conflicts, universe knowledge offers tools to navigate life with grace and effectiveness.

This chapter bridges theory and practice, showing you how to incorporate universe knowledge into your daily routine to enhance creativity, decision-making, and relationships.

CHAPTER SEVEN: APPLYING UNIVERSE KNOWLEDGE IN EVERYDAY LIFE

Expanding Your Knowledge Base

To harness universe knowledge, it's essential to cultivate curiosity and seek understanding across various dimensions of life:

1. Explore Different Disciplines

Broaden your perspective by studying diverse fields, including science, history, philosophy, and spirituality. Each discipline offers unique insights that, when combined, create a holistic understanding of the world.

Examples:
- Learning about ecosystems from biology reveals the interconnectedness of life.

- Studying philosophy encourages critical thinking and ethical reasoning.

- Spiritual practices like mindfulness promote emotional clarity and presence.

Actionable Tip: *Dedicate 30 minutes daily to learning something new—read a book, watch a documentary, or take an online course. Over time, this habit builds a foundation for informed and intuitive decision-making.*

2. Learn from Others

Mentors, peers, and even casual conversations can serve as valuable sources of wisdom.

How to Engage:
- **Mentors:** Seek guidance from people with experience in areas you wish to grow.

- **Group Discussions:** Join book clubs, professional forums, or spiritual gatherings to exchange ideas.

- **Active Listening:** Approach conversations with humility and a willingness to learn.

Example: *A casual chat with a colleague about time management could reveal strategies you hadn't considered, enhancing your productivity.*

Practicing Mindfulness and Reflection

1. Meditation and Presence
Mindfulness practices help you quiet mental noise, allowing intuitive insights to surface.

Practical Exercise:
- Begin your day with a 5-minute meditation. Focus on your breath or a calming image, such as waves gently lapping the shore. This practice sets a tone of clarity and focus.

CHAPTER SEVEN: APPLYING UNIVERSE KNOWLEDGE IN EVERYDAY LIFE

2. Journaling
Reflective journaling helps organize your thoughts, uncover patterns, and process emotions.

Prompts to Try:
- What challenged me today, and what did I learn from it?

- What intuitive ideas arose today, and how can I act on them?

- What am I grateful for at this moment?

Over time, journaling reveals connections between your actions, feelings, and outcomes, guiding you toward intentional growth.

Using Universe Knowledge for Decision-Making

When faced with decisions, apply a balanced approach:

Step 1: Gather Information
Use logical thinking to analyze facts and weigh options.

Step 2: Trust Your Intuition
Once you've considered the data, quiet your mind and tune into your instincts. Intuition often synthesizes information in ways your conscious mind cannot.

Example: *If deciding between two job offers, research the roles (thinking), then visualize yourself in each position and notice which feels more aligned with your values (thought).*

Enhancing Creativity with Universe Knowledge

Creativity thrives when you balance structure with spontaneity, drawing from universal principles to inspire innovation.

Practical Strategies:
1. **Seek Inspiration:** Expose yourself to diverse perspectives. A painter might study architecture for ideas on structure, while a writer might explore music to spark emotional resonance.

2. **Relax to Create:** Many creative breakthroughs happen during moments of relaxation. Step away from the task and engage in activities like walking, listening to music, or meditating to let intuitive ideas emerge.

3. **Experiment Freely:** Treat mistakes as stepping stones. When you explore without fear of failure, you invite innovation.

Example: *Thomas Edison famously experimented with thousands of materials before inventing the lightbulb, demonstrating persistence and a willingness to adapt.*

Building Stronger Relationships

Universe knowledge teaches us that relationships thrive on empathy, communication, and understanding.

1. Practice Empathy
Empathy bridges gaps by helping you see the world from another's perspective.

Exercise: *During conversations, focus entirely on the other person. Listen without formulating a response and reflect back on what you've understood.*

2. Resolve Conflicts Thoughtfully
Approach disagreements with a mindset of curiosity rather than judgment. Ask open-ended questions like, "What's most important to you in this situation?"

Example: A misunderstanding with a coworker might stem from different communication styles. By empathizing and asking clarifying questions, you can uncover shared goals and work toward a solution.

Living with a Growth Mindset

A growth mindset—a belief in the potential to learn and evolve—aligns closely with universe knowledge.

Ways to Cultivate a Growth Mindset:
1. **Reframe Challenges:** *View setbacks as opportunities to grow.*

2. **Celebrate Progress:** *Acknowledge small victories to stay motivated.*

3. **Stay Curious:** *Treat each day as a chance to discover something new.*

Example: *After facing a failed project, instead of giving up, reflect on what went wrong and identify lessons to apply to future efforts.*

Key Insights

1. Expand your knowledge through diverse disciplines, conversations, and personal reflection.

2. Mindfulness and journaling create clarity, revealing patterns and fostering intuitive insights.

3. Balanced decision-making combines logical analysis with intuitive guidance.

4. Creativity thrives when you embrace experimentation, relaxation, and inspiration.

5. Strong relationships are built on empathy, thoughtful communication, and conflict resolution.

6. Adopting a growth mindset ensures continuous learning and resilience in the face of challenges.

Reflection Questions

1. What steps can you take to expand your knowledge in areas like science, philosophy, or spirituality?

2. How might mindfulness practices, like meditation or journaling, improve your decision-making?

3. Reflect on a time when intuition helped you make the right choice. How did you recognize it?

4. What new experiences or creative practices could inspire innovation in your work or personal life?

5. How can you approach your relationships with more empathy and understanding?

CHAPTER 8

THE SYNERGY OF THINKING AND THOUGHT

THINKING VS THOUGHT

Picture yourself solving a puzzle. You carefully analyze each piece, examining shapes and colors to figure out where they fit. Just as you're stumped, you suddenly spot the perfect piece without consciously searching for it. That moment of clarity isn't random—it's the synergy of thinking (logical problem-solving) and thought (intuitive insight) working together.

This chapter explores how the balance of thinking and thought can elevate your creativity, decision-making, and problem-solving, offering practical strategies to integrate these processes into your daily life.

CHAPTER EIGHT: THE SYNERGY OF THINKING AND THOUGHT

Understanding the Synergy

The Role of Thinking

Thinking involves conscious, logical analysis. It's methodical, helping you plan, strategize, and evaluate. For example, writing a business proposal requires structured thinking to gather data, outline arguments, and address potential challenges.

The Role of Thought

Thought, on the other hand, is intuitive and spontaneous. It often arises in moments of stillness or relaxation when the mind isn't actively focused. A sudden idea for a new project or an unexpected insight during a walk illustrates the power of thought.

Key Point: *Thinking lays the groundwork, while thought provides the creative spark. When used together, they create a dynamic partnership that unlocks greater potential.*

How Thinking and Thought Work Together

The Complementary Process
- **Thinking Constructs:** It organizes, evaluates, and applies structure.

- **Thought Connects:** It identifies patterns, inspires innovation, and fosters creativity.

Example: *Planning a trip involves both processes. Thinking helps you research flights, book accommodations, and create a schedule. Thought might inspire you to explore an off-the-beaten-path destination or try a local experience that wasn't in the original plan. Together, they ensure the trip is both organized and memorable.*

Cultivating Balance Between Thinking and Thought

1. Alternate Between Focus and Relaxation
Thinking thrives during focused effort, while thought flourishes in moments of rest. Shifting between these states allows your mind to process information deeply and uncover intuitive insights.

Practical Exercise:
- Set aside dedicated time for concentrated work.

- Follow this with a relaxing activity, like a walk or meditation, to give your subconscious space to process and generate ideas.

2. Embrace Iterative Problem-Solving
Start with structured planning, then refine your approach as intuitive insights emerge.

Example: *An artist might sketch a detailed outline (thinking) but experiment with colors or composition spontaneously (thought) as the work progresses. This back-and-forth creates a balance between precision and creativity.*

3. Use Visualization to Bridge Thinking and Thought
Visualization activates both analytical and intuitive faculties, helping you create a mental blueprint while leaving room for inspiration.

Exercise: *Before tackling a project, close your eyes and imagine the steps required to complete it. Allow space for unexpected ideas or solutions to surface.*

Practical Applications of Thinking and Thought

1. Creativity
Creative pursuits often require a balance of planning and improvisation. Writers, for instance, may outline a story (thinking) but let characters or plot twists evolve naturally as they write (thought).

Example: *Lin-Manuel Miranda, creator of Hamilton, used historical research (thinking) to ground his work but relied on inspiration and intuition (thought) to compose its groundbreaking music and lyrics.*

2. Decision-Making
Important decisions benefit from logical evaluation paired with intuitive guidance.

Example: When deciding on a career move, analyze pros and cons (thinking), but also reflect on which choice feels more aligned with your values and aspirations (thought).

3. Relationships
In communication, thinking ensures clarity and fairness, while thought helps you sense unspoken emotions or underlying dynamics.

Example: *During a disagreement, thinking might help you articulate your point logically, while thought allows you to empathize and adjust your tone to foster understanding.*

Overcoming Imbalances

Too Much Thinking
Overthinking can lead to analysis paralysis, where you become stuck in a cycle of indecision.

Solution:
- Take a break and engage in a creative or physical activity to disrupt the cycle.

- Remind yourself that not every decision requires exhaustive analysis—sometimes a gut feeling is enough.

Too Much Thought
Relying solely on intuition without grounding in logic can result in impulsive or poorly thought-out actions.

CHAPTER EIGHT: THE SYNERGY OF THINKING AND THOUGHT

Solution:
- Pause to evaluate your intuitive ideas. Ask, "Is this practical? What steps would make this actionable?"

- Use thinking to test and refine your instincts.

Building the Synergy Through Daily Practices

1. **Journaling:** Reflect on challenges or projects, alternating between logical analysis and brainstorming. This practice strengthens your ability to switch between modes.

2. **Meditation:** Regular meditation quiets the mind, creating space for thought to emerge naturally and complement structured thinking.

3. **Set Time for Play:** Unstructured, playful activities (like doodling, dancing, or tinkering) encourage creativity and intuitive problem-solving.

4. **Mindful Pauses:** Throughout the day, take short breaks to tune into your instincts. Ask yourself, "What feels right in this moment?"

Key Insights

1. Thinking provides structure, while thought introduces creativity and spontaneity. Both are essential for effective problem-solving and decision-making.

2. Alternating between focus and relaxation creates a rhythm that supports deeper insights.

3. Visualization bridges thinking and thought, allowing you to combine logical planning with intuitive inspiration.

4. Overthinking leads to stagnation, while unchecked intuition risks impulsiveness. Strive for balance by integrating these processes intentionally.

Reflection Questions

1. Can you think of a time when logical planning and intuitive inspiration worked together to achieve a goal? How did this synergy help?

2. Do you tend to rely more on thinking or thought? How might you practice balancing these processes?

3. How can you use activities like journaling, meditation, or play to strengthen the connection between thinking and thought?

4. Reflect on a recent decision. How did thinking and thought each influence your choice?

5. What strategies could you implement to overcome overthinking or impulsiveness in your daily life?

CHAPTER 9
BALANCING THINKING AND THOUGHT

*Imagine trying to balance on a tightrope. Lean too far in one direction, and you'll fall; lean too far in the other, and the same thing happens. This act mirrors the balance between **thinking** and **thought**. When you rely too much on thinking, you risk getting trapped in over analysis. When you depend solely on thought, you may act impulsively. The key is finding the middle ground, where logic and intuition work together in harmony.*

This chapter explores how emotions influence this balance and how developing emotional intelligence can help you achieve clarity, resilience, and effectiveness in decision-making.

The Emotional Link to Thinking and Thought

How Emotions Shape Thinking

Emotions can enhance or distort logical thinking. Positive emotions like excitement or joy can fuel creativity and problem-solving, while negative emotions like fear or anger may cloud judgment.

Example: *During a stressful situation, anxiety might push you into overthinking, causing indecision. On the other hand, calmness can create the mental clarity needed to analyze options effectively.*

How Emotions Influence Thought

Thought is deeply tied to intuition, which often emerges from emotional cues. For instance, a gut feeling might arise because your subconscious mind recognizes patterns your conscious mind hasn't yet processed.

Example: *Imagine meeting someone for the first time and feeling an immediate sense of trust or unease. This intuitive reaction is shaped by subtle emotional signals, such as tone, body language, or past experiences.*

Key Point: *Emotional awareness is critical to balancing thinking and thought. Recognizing how emotions impact these processes helps you channel them productively.*

Developing Emotional Intelligence for Balance

1. Self-Awareness
Self-awareness is the ability to recognize and understand your emotions as they arise. It's the foundation for managing emotions and maintaining balance.

Practical Exercise:
- Throughout the day, pause and ask yourself, "What am I feeling right now? How is this affecting my thoughts and actions?"

- Use journaling to reflect on emotional patterns, such as how frustration might lead to overthinking or how joy fosters spontaneity.

2. Self-Regulation
Once you're aware of your emotions, self-regulation allows you to manage them effectively. This involves transforming negative emotions into constructive energy.

Techniques:
- **Deep Breathing:** When overwhelmed, take slow, deep breaths to calm your nervous system.

- **Reframing:** Replace limiting thoughts like "I'm stuck" with empowering ones like "This is an opportunity to learn."

- **Pause Before Acting:** When emotions feel intense, step back and give yourself time to respond thoughtfully.

Empathy: Understanding Others' Emotions

Empathy, the ability to understand and share others' emotions, enhances your ability to connect with people and navigate relationships.

Practical Example: *In a team setting, recognizing a colleague's frustration can help you adjust your approach, creating space for collaboration rather than conflict.*

Empathy Exercise:
- During a conversation, focus entirely on listening. Avoid interrupting or planning your response. Afterward, reflect on what the person's words and emotions reveal about their perspective.

Resilience: Adapting to Setbacks

Resilience is the ability to recover from difficulties and maintain emotional balance in the face of challenges. Resilient individuals can adapt their thinking and thought processes to respond effectively, rather than reacting impulsively or becoming paralyzed by over analysis.

Example: *After receiving critical feedback at work, a resilient person might reflect on the constructive aspects (thinking) while trusting their intuition to guide improvements (thought).*

Building Resilience:

1. **Cultivate Gratitude:** Focus on positive aspects of your life to shift your mindset.

2. **Focus on Solutions:** Instead of dwelling on the problem, channel energy into actionable steps.

3. **Visualize Success:** Imagine overcoming the challenge and how it will feel.

Common Imbalances and How to Correct Them

1. Overthinking
Symptoms:
- Difficulty making decisions.
- Replaying scenarios in your mind without resolution.

Solutions:
- Limit decision-making time. For example, give yourself 10 minutes to choose an option and commit to it.
- Practice mindfulness to quiet mental chatter.

2. Impulsiveness
Symptoms:
- Acting without considering consequences.
- Overreliance on gut feelings.

Solutions:
- Use the "pause and plan" method: Take a moment to evaluate options before acting.

- Write down pros and cons to ensure your intuition aligns with logic.

Practical Tools for Balance

1. Meditation for Clarity
Meditation helps calm emotional turbulence, creating space for both thinking and thought to operate effectively.

Simple Practice:
- Sit in a quiet space and focus on your breath for 5–10 minutes. If thoughts arise, acknowledge them without judgment and return to your breath.

2. Visualization for Decision-Making
Use visualization to combine logical planning with intuitive insight.

Exercise:
- Picture yourself successfully navigating a situation. Visualize the steps needed to achieve the outcome and remain open to spontaneous ideas that emerge.

3. Journaling for Reflection
Journaling helps process emotions, identify patterns, and evaluate decisions.

Prompts to Try:
- What emotions influenced my decisions today?

- Did I overthink or act impulsively? How can I adjust next time?

Key Insights

1. Emotional awareness is critical to balancing thinking and thought, as emotions influence both processes.

2. Developing self-regulation skills helps you manage emotions, avoiding extremes like overthinking or impulsiveness.

3. Empathy strengthens relationships by fostering understanding and connection.

4. Resilience transforms setbacks into opportunities for growth, promoting balance and clarity.

5. Practical tools like meditation, visualization, and journaling enhance emotional intelligence, supporting harmony between thinking and thought.

Reflection Questions

1. How do your emotions typically influence your thinking and thought processes? Can you identify patterns that help or hinder balance?

2. Reflect on a recent decision. Did you overthink or act impulsively? How could you approach similar situations differently?

3. How might self-awareness and self-regulation improve your emotional balance in daily life?

4. Think of a time when empathy helped you navigate a conflict or deepen a connection. What did you learn from that experience?

5. How do you currently handle setbacks? What practices, like gratitude or visualization, could help you build resilience?

CHAPTER 10

THE ROLE OF PRESENCE IN UNLOCKING UNIVERSE KNOWLEDGE

Think about the last time you felt truly present—fully immersed in the moment, without distractions. Maybe it was during a heartfelt conversation, watching a sunset, or losing yourself in a creative project. In these moments, you weren't stuck in overthinking or rushing impulsively. Instead, you were connected to something deeper—a flow of clarity, creativity, and intuition.

Presence is the gateway to universe knowledge. This chapter explores how cultivating presence allows you to access universal wisdom, quiet mental noise, and create a foundation for balanced thinking and thought.

CHAPTER TEN: THE ROLE OF PRESENCE INUNLOCKING UNIVERSE KNOWLEDGE

What Does It Mean to Be Present?

Presence is more than simply being in the moment—it's a state of full awareness and engagement with your surroundings, free from distractions of the past or future.

Key Characteristics of Presence:

1. **Awareness:** Fully noticing your thoughts, emotions, and sensations without judgment.

2. **Focus:** Giving your undivided attention to the current moment.

3. **Connection:** Feeling attuned to your environment and the people around you.

Example: *Imagine walking through a forest. If you're present, you notice the crunch of leaves underfoot, the chirping of birds, and the crispness of the air. If you're distracted, your mind is elsewhere, and you miss the richness of the experience.*

Why Presence Is Vital for Universe Knowledge

Presence acts as a bridge between logical thinking and intuitive thought, allowing you to:

- **Quiet Mental Chatter:** By focusing on the now, you reduce overthinking and create space for intuition to emerge.

- **Strengthen Perception:** Presence heightens your awareness of subtle details and patterns, making it easier to recognize insights.

- **Enhance Decision-Making:** When present, you're less likely to be influenced by fear, distraction, or impulsiveness, enabling clearer and wiser choices.

Barriers to Presence

1. Overthinking
Constant mental chatter keeps you stuck in analysis, preventing you from fully experiencing the moment.

Solution:
Practice mindfulness techniques to redirect your focus to the present, such as concentrating on your breath or physical sensations.

2. Multitasking
Attempting to do too many things at once fractures your attention and reduces your ability to engage deeply.

Solution:
Adopt a single-tasking approach. Commit to one activity at a time, whether it's eating, working, or having a conversation.

3. Technology and Distractions
Devices like smartphones pull you away from the present with constant notifications and information overload.

Solution:
Set boundaries for technology use, such as designated screen-free times or zones.

Practices to Cultivate Presence

1. Mindful Breathing
Breathing exercises anchor you to the present by focusing your attention on a simple, repetitive action.

Exercise:
- Inhale deeply for a count of four.
- Hold your breath for a count of four.
- Exhale slowly for a count of six.

Repeat this cycle 3–5 times, noticing the sensations of your breath as it moves through your body.

2. Grounding Techniques
Grounding involves using your senses to connect with the physical world around you.

Exercise:
- Name five things you can see.
- Identify four things you can touch.
- Listen for three things you can hear.
- Notice two things you can smell.

- Pay attention to one thing you can taste.

This exercise brings you into the present by shifting your focus to your immediate environment.

3. The Power of Pausing
In the middle of a busy day, pausing to center yourself creates opportunities for presence.

Example: *Before responding to an email, take a moment to breathe, clarify your intention, and approach the task with full attention.*

Presence in Daily Life

1. Relationships
When present in conversations, you listen actively, pick up on emotional cues, and respond thoughtfully. This fosters deeper connections and reduces misunderstandings.

Example: *During a discussion with a friend, instead of planning your response, focus entirely on what they're saying. Reflect back what you've heard to ensure understanding.*

2. Creativity and Work
Presence enhances flow states, where you lose track of time and work with heightened focus and creativity.

Example: *A writer who clears distractions and focuses on the act of writing—without worrying about perfection—produces more authentic and inspired work.*

3. Stress Management

Presence reduces stress by shifting your attention from overwhelming worries to the reality of the moment.

Example: *In a stressful situation, pause and ground yourself using mindful breathing. Ask, "What can I influence right now?"*

How Presence Unlocks Universe Knowledge

When you cultivate presence, you create the ideal conditions for universe knowledge to flow:

- **Reduced Noise:** A quiet mind allows intuitive thoughts to surface.

- **Heightened Awareness:** By tuning into subtle details, you're more likely to notice patterns and insights.

- **Connection to Universal Energy:** Presence fosters a sense of interconnectedness, aligning you with the wisdom of the universe.

Illustration: *A scientist struggling with a complex problem might step away for a moment of stillness. In this state of presence, a breakthrough idea may emerge—one that feels effortless and profound.*

Common Misconceptions About Presence

1. "Being Present Means Doing Nothing"
Presence doesn't mean inactivity—it means engaging fully with whatever you're doing.

2. "I Don't Have Time to Be Present"
Presence isn't about setting aside hours for mindfulness. Even brief moments of presence—like focusing on your breath for 10 seconds—can make a significant difference.

3. "Presence Is Only for Relaxation"
While presence is calming, it's also a tool for action, enabling clarity, focus, and intuitive decision-making.

·········· **Key Insights** ··········

1. Presence is the state of full awareness and engagement in the moment, free from distractions.

2. Cultivating presence enhances clarity, creativity, and decision-making by balancing thinking and thought.

3. Barriers like overthinking, multitasking, and distractions can be overcome through mindfulness practices, grounding techniques, and pauses.

4. Presence transforms relationships, creativity, and stress management by fostering deeper connection and focus.

5. Presence creates the ideal conditions for universe knowledge to flow, enabling intuitive insights and a sense of interconnectedness.

Reflection Questions

1. Reflect on a recent experience where you felt fully present. What made that moment special?

2. How do distractions like multitasking or technology impact your ability to be present?

3. Which mindfulness or grounding practices could you incorporate into your daily routine to cultivate presence?

4. How might being more present improve your relationships, work, or personal well-being?

5. What steps can you take to create more opportunities for presence in your daily life?

CHAPTER 11

TRUSTING THE FLOW OF UNIVERSE KNOWLEDGE

THINKING VS THOUGHT

Have you ever noticed how life seems to flow effortlessly when you're in sync with your intuition? Decisions feel natural, opportunities appear at just the right time, and challenges resolve with unexpected ease. This isn't luck—it's the result of aligning with universe knowledge.

Trusting the flow of universe knowledge means releasing the need to control every detail and embracing a sense of surrender to life's natural rhythms. In this chapter, we'll explore how trust amplifies your connection to universal wisdom and how to navigate life with confidence and grace.

CHAPTER ELEVEN: TRUSTING THE FLOW OF UNIVERSE KNOWLEDGE

What Does It Mean to Trust the Flow?

Trusting the flow involves allowing universe knowledge to guide your actions, even when the path forward isn't immediately clear. It requires balancing preparation with openness, making space for intuitive insights to shape your journey.

Key Elements of Trusting the Flow:

1. **Letting Go of Control:** Accepting that not everything can be planned or predicted.

2. **Staying Open to Possibilities:** Being receptive to unexpected opportunities or solutions.

3. **Acting with Intention:** Combining thoughtful preparation with intuitive action.

Example: *A writer experiencing creative block might initially feel frustrated, forcing ideas that don't resonate. By stepping back and trusting the process, they might suddenly find inspiration during a walk or conversation.*

The Science of Trust and Flow

Flow State and the Brain

The concept of flow—a state of deep focus and effortless action—is closely linked to trusting universe knowledge. Neuroscientists have found that during flow states:

- The prefrontal cortex (responsible for overthinking) quiets down, allowing intuitive thought to dominate.

- Dopamine levels increase, enhancing creativity and motivation.

- The brain synchronizes, leading to heightened focus and performance.

Practical Insight: *Flow states arise when you balance challenge and skill, fully immersing yourself in the task at hand while letting go of distractions and doubts.*

Barriers to Trusting the Flow

1. Fear of Uncertainty
Many people struggle to trust the flow because they fear losing control. This fear creates resistance, blocking access to intuitive insights.

Solution:
Reframe uncertainty as a space for growth and discovery. Instead of focusing on what might go wrong, ask, "What opportunities could arise from this situation?"

2. Perfectionism
The need for perfection often leads to overplanning and hesitation, disrupting the flow.

Solution:
Adopt a mindset of progress over perfection. Trust that even imperfect actions can lead to valuable lessons and outcomes.

3. Impatience
Trying to rush the process can result in forced decisions that feel unnatural or misaligned.

Solution: Practice patience by focusing on small, consistent steps. Trust that the right outcomes will emerge in their own time.

How to Strengthen Trust in the Flow

1. Set Clear Intentions
Clarity of purpose creates a framework for universe knowledge to guide you. While you don't need to control every detail, having a clear vision helps direct your energy.

Exercise:
- Write down your intention for a specific area of life (e.g., "I want to find meaningful work that aligns with my values").
- Reflect on this intention daily, remaining open to how it unfolds.

2. Listen to Intuition
Your intuition acts as a compass, pointing you toward aligned actions.

Practice:
- Start with small decisions, like choosing what to eat or wear. Pay attention to the options that "feel right."

- Gradually apply intuition to larger decisions, like career moves or relationships, combining it with logical thinking.

3. Embrace Stillness
Stillness creates space for intuitive insights to emerge. Practices like meditation or spending time in nature quiet the mind, making it easier to tune into the flow.

Exercise:
- Spend 10 minutes in silence each day. Focus on your breath or the sounds around you, and notice any thoughts or ideas that arise naturally.

4. Take Aligned Action
Trusting the flow doesn't mean being passive—it involves acting when opportunities feel aligned with your intuition and purpose.

Example: *If you feel drawn to reach out to someone or explore a new opportunity, act on that impulse. Often, these small actions lead to surprising and meaningful outcomes.*

CHAPTER ELEVEN: TRUSTING THE FLOW OF UNIVERSE KNOWLEDGE

The Role of Surrender in Trusting the Flow

Surrender doesn't mean giving up; it means letting go of unnecessary resistance and trusting the process. This mindset allows you to adapt to challenges and embrace uncertainty without losing momentum.

How to Practice Surrender:
1. **Detach from Specific Outcomes:** Focus on the journey rather than fixating on how things "should" unfold.

2. **Trust Timing:** Understand that delays or detours might be necessary for growth or better opportunities.

3. **Celebrate Progress:** Acknowledge small wins along the way, reinforcing your faith in the process.

Stories of Trusting the Flow

1. The Unplanned Opportunity
A young entrepreneur, frustrated with their stagnant career, decides to volunteer for a local event. Through this experience, they meet a mentor who offers invaluable guidance, leading to unexpected success.

Lesson: *Opportunities often arise when you let go of rigid plans and follow your intuition.*

2. The Unexpected Solution
A scientist struggling with a complex problem decides to take a break and spend time outdoors. During a moment of stillness,

they suddenly realize a new approach that had eluded them for weeks.

Lesson: *Stillness and trust often pave the way for breakthroughs.*

Practical Tools for Trusting the Flow

1. Affirmations for Trust
Repeat affirmations to reinforce trust in yourself and the universe. Examples:

- "I trust the process of life."
- "I am open to unexpected opportunities."
- "The universe is working in my favor."

2. Visualization
Imagine yourself navigating life with ease and confidence, trusting that the right people, opportunities, and solutions will come your way.

3. Gratitude Practice
Focusing on what's working well reinforces trust in the flow. Each day, write down three things you're grateful for, no matter how small.

Key Insights

1. Trusting the flow of universe knowledge involves balancing preparation with openness to intuition.

2. Fear, perfectionism, and impatience are common barriers to trust, but they can be overcome with mindset shifts and practices like stillness and reflection.

3. Flow states arise when you let go of resistance and immerse yourself fully in the moment, allowing universal wisdom to guide you.

4. Surrendering control doesn't mean passivity—it means embracing uncertainty and acting on aligned opportunities.

5. Practical tools like affirmations, visualization, and gratitude strengthen your ability to trust the process and navigate life with confidence.

Reflection Questions

1. Reflect on a time when trusting your intuition led to a positive outcome. What made that experience successful?

2. How do fear or perfectionism show up in your life, and how might they block you from trusting the flow?

3. What small steps can you take to practice surrender and embrace uncertainty?

4. How could daily affirmations or gratitude practices help you reinforce trust in yourself and the universe?

5. What area of your life would benefit most from trusting the flow of universe knowledge right now?

CHAPTER 12

THE ROLE OF ACTION IN

THINKING VS THOUGHT

Imagine standing at the edge of a vast ocean. You've spent time observing the waves, studying the tides, and learning about their currents. But the real understanding—the kind that can only be felt—comes when you step into the water. Universe knowledge works the same way: it's not just something you think or feel; it's something you act on.

This chapter explores the importance of action as a catalyst for accessing and applying universe knowledge, showing how deliberate, aligned steps bridge the gap between insight and impact.

Why Action Is Essential

While reflection and intuition are powerful tools, they only gain meaning when translated into purposeful action. Action gives life to ideas, turning abstract concepts into tangible results.

Key Principles of Action:

1. **Action Clarifies Insight:** Taking the first step often reveals information or opportunities that weren't visible before.

2. **Action Strengthens Intuition:** Repeatedly acting on intuitive nudges builds trust in your inner guidance.

3. **Action Creates Momentum:** Even small steps generate energy that propels you forward.

Example: *Consider someone who feels inspired to author a book. Reflecting on the idea is valuable, but the true journey begins when they start outlining chapters or drafting pages.*

The Relationship Between Thought and Action

Thought Inspires Action

Intuitive insights often point you in the right direction, offering a vision or spark of inspiration. Acting on these insights validates them, creating a cycle of trust and growth.

Action Generates New Thoughts

Each action provides feedback, deepening your understanding and refining your approach.

Example: *A business owner might intuitively sense a market need and act by launching a new product. Feedback from customers then helps them adjust and improve.*

Overcoming Barriers to Action

1. Fear of Failure
Fear of making mistakes often paralyzes people, keeping them from taking the first step.

Solution: *Reframe failure as a learning opportunity. Each misstep provides valuable insights that guide you closer to success.*

2. Perfectionism
Waiting for the "perfect" moment or plan can lead to endless delays.

Solution: *Adopt the principle of progress over perfection. Start small and refine as you go.*

3. Doubt in Intuition
Lack of trust in intuitive guidance can lead to hesitation or second-guessing.

Solution: *Begin with low-stakes actions based on intuition to build confidence. Reflect on the outcomes to strengthen your trust.*

The Power of Small Steps

Taking small, consistent actions is often more effective than waiting for one grand leap.

Benefits of Small Steps:
1. **Manageable:** They feel less intimidating, making it easier to start.

2. **Flexible:** You can adapt your approach based on feedback.

3. **Momentum-Building:** Successes from small steps create confidence and motivation.

Example: *If someone dreams of starting a nonprofit, their first small step might be researching similar organizations or volunteering in the field. These small actions build experience and clarity.*

Aligning Action with Universe Knowledge

1. Act on Intuitive Nudges
When an idea or gut feeling resonates deeply, take action—no matter how small.

Example: *You might feel an unexplained urge to reconnect with an old friend. Acting on this nudge could lead to a meaningful opportunity or lesson.*

2. Reflect on Feedback
After taking action, pause to evaluate the results. This reflection helps refine your approach and strengthens your connection to universe knowledge.

Exercise:

- What went well?

- What did you learn?

- What could you do differently next time?

3. Trust Timing
Universe knowledge often operates on its own schedule. Acting too soon or waiting too long can disrupt the flow.

Practical Tip: *Combine thoughtful preparation with patience. When an opportunity feels aligned, act decisively without hesitation.*

Action in Different Areas of Life

1. Relationships
Taking action in relationships—like initiating a conversation or offering support—fosters connection and understanding.

Example: *If you sense a friend is struggling, acting on that intuition by reaching out can deepen your bond and provide timely help.*

2. Creativity
Creativity thrives on experimentation. Acting on an idea, even imperfectly, creates momentum and inspires further innovation.

Example: *A painter might start with rough sketches, allowing intuition to guide the evolution of the final piece.*

3. Career and Goals
Professional growth often requires bold action, such as pursuing a new opportunity or advocating for yourself.

Example: *If you feel drawn to a particular field, taking steps like networking or acquiring new skills aligns your actions with your deeper purpose.*

The Role of Faith in Action

Taking action requires faith—not only in yourself but also in the process of life. Faith bridges the gap between uncertainty and confidence, allowing you to act despite fear or doubt.

How to Cultivate Faith in Action:
1. **Visualize Success:** Imagine the positive outcomes of your actions to reinforce confidence.

2. **Acknowledge Past Wins:** Reflect on times when taking action led to growth or opportunity.

3. **Embrace Uncertainty:** Recognize that not knowing the full path is part of the journey.

Practical Exercises for Taking Aligned Action

1. The 3-Action Rule
Identify a goal or intention and write down three small actions you can take today to move toward it.

Example: *If your goal is to improve your health, your three actions might include drinking more water, taking a 20-minute walk, and preparing a healthy meal.*

2. Morning Intention Setting
Start each day by setting an intention and identifying one action to support it.

Example: *Intention: "I will approach today with curiosity."*

Action: *"I'll ask open-ended questions during meetings to learn from others."*

3. Weekly Reflection and Adjustment
At the end of each week, review the actions you've taken and assess their impact. Use this feedback to plan your next steps.

Key Insights

1. Action is the bridge between insight and impact, giving life to intuitive ideas and reflections.

2. Small, consistent actions build momentum and provide valuable feedback, helping refine your path.

3. Common barriers like fear, perfectionism, and doubt can be overcome through mindset shifts and simple strategies.

4. Aligning action with intuitive nudges and universe knowledge creates a sense of flow and purpose.

5. Faith in the process is essential for taking bold, aligned steps, even in the face of uncertainty.

Reflection Questions

1. What's a small action you could take today to move closer to a goal or intention?

2. Reflect on a time when taking action—no matter how small—led to a meaningful outcome. What did you learn?

3. How do fear or perfectionism hold you back from acting on your ideas? What strategies could help you overcome these barriers?

4. How can you use reflection and feedback to refine your actions and align them more closely with your intuition?

5. In what area of your life do you feel called to take bold, aligned action? What's the first step?

CHAPTER 13
LIVING IN ALIGNMENT WITH UNIVERSE KNOWLEDGE

Have you ever experienced a moment where everything seemed to fall into place—a decision felt effortless, an opportunity appeared at just the right time, or your actions flowed seamlessly? These moments are the result of living in alignment with universe knowledge. When your thoughts, emotions, and actions harmonize with the deeper rhythms of life, you unlock a state of ease, clarity, and fulfillment.

In this chapter, we'll explore how to create a lifestyle aligned with universe knowledge, ensuring that your daily choices reflect your higher purpose and intuitive wisdom.

CHAPTER THIRTEEN: LIVING IN ALIGNMENT WITH UNIVERSE KNOWLEDGE

What Does Alignment Mean?

Alignment occurs when your actions, values, and intuition are in sync with the flow of universal principles. It's about living authentically, making choices that reflect who you truly are, and allowing universe knowledge to guide your journey.

Signs of Alignment:

- You feel energized and purposeful.

- Decisions come naturally, with less overthinking.

- Challenges are met with resilience and trust.

- You experience synchronicities, such as chance meetings or timely opportunities.

Example: *A musician who aligns with their passion for creating art feels deeply fulfilled, even in the face of challenges, because their actions are rooted in authenticity and purpose.*

How Misalignment Happens

Misalignment occurs when fear, external pressures, or distractions pull you away from your true path.

Common Causes:
1. **Ignoring Intuition:** Overriding gut feelings in favor of logic or societal expectations.

2. **Chasing External Validation:** Prioritizing approval or material success over internal fulfillment.

3. **Disconnection from Values:** Losing sight of what truly matters to you.

Example: *A professional might stay in a high-paying job they dislike, ignoring their inner calling to pursue a more meaningful career. Over time, this misalignment leads to stress, dissatisfaction, and burnout.*

The Benefits of Alignment

Living in alignment with universe knowledge transforms your experience of life:

- **Clarity:** You make decisions with confidence, guided by your intuition and values.

- **Ease:** Life flows more smoothly as you align with universal rhythms.

- **Fulfillment:** Your actions reflect your authentic self, creating a sense of purpose and joy.

Example: *A teacher who values connection and growth feels a deep sense of purpose when helping students discover their potential. This alignment brings energy and satisfaction to their work.*

Practical Steps to Live in Alignment

1. Clarify Your Core Values
Understanding what matters most to you provides a foundation for aligned living.

Exercise:
- Write down your top five values (e.g., creativity, integrity, freedom, connection, growth).

- Reflect on how your current actions support or conflict with these values.

Example: *If creativity is a core value, but your daily routine lacks opportunities for expression, consider making time for activities like painting, writing, or brainstorming.*

2. Listen to Your Intuition
Intuition is a key component of alignment, offering guidance that aligns with your authentic self.

Practical Tip:
- Start with small decisions (e.g., what to eat, how to spend free time) and act on the choice that feels most natural.

- Gradually extend this practice to bigger decisions, such as career moves or relationships.

3. Align Your Actions with Your Intentions
Intentions set the direction, but actions bring alignment to life.

Exercise:
Each morning, set an intention that reflects your values and purpose (e.g., "I will approach today with kindness and curiosity"). Throughout the day, take actions that reinforce this intention.

Example: *If your intention is to cultivate kindness, you might offer a compliment to a coworker or practice patience in a challenging situation.*

4. Practice Mindful Decision-Making
Mindfulness helps you evaluate whether your choices align with your intuition and values.

Decision-Making Questions to Ask:
- Does this choice reflect my authentic self?

- Does it feel right in my gut?

- Will it bring me closer to my long-term goals and purpose?

Example: *Before accepting a new opportunity, take a moment to assess whether it aligns with your vision for the future.*

Overcoming Challenges to Alignment

1. External Pressures
Society, family, or peers may encourage choices that conflict with your intuition.

Solution:
- Set boundaries to protect your values and priorities.

- Surround yourself with supportive individuals who respect your path.

2. Fear of Change
Alignment often requires stepping into the unknown, which can feel intimidating.

Solution:
- Focus on small, manageable changes.

- Remind yourself that growth happens outside your comfort zone.

3. Doubt in Intuition
When you second-guess your inner guidance, you may hesitate to act.

Solution:
- Keep an intuition journal to track decisions made based on gut feelings and their outcomes. Over time, this practice builds confidence in your intuition.

Living Aligned Across Life's Dimensions

1. Relationships
Aligned relationships prioritize authenticity, mutual respect, and shared values.

Example: *Rather than staying in a relationship out of obligation, focus on connections that feel genuine and uplifting.*

2. Career
Aligned work reflects your passions and strengths, contributing to a sense of purpose.

Example: *If you value freedom, consider careers that allow for flexibility and independence.*

3. Daily Habits
Your routines and habits should support your physical, emotional, and spiritual well-being.

Example: *If health is a priority, create a routine that includes nutritious meals, regular exercise, and mindfulness practices.*

Signs You're Living in Alignment

1. **Inner Peace:** You feel calm and centered, even during challenges.

2. **Synchronicities:** Meaningful coincidences occur, confirming you're on the right path.

CHAPTER THIRTEEN: LIVING IN ALIGNMENT WITH UNIVERSE KNOWLEDGE

3. **Sustained Energy:** You feel motivated and engaged, even when working hard.

4. **Resilience:** You bounce back quickly from setbacks, trusting the process of life.

Key Insights

1. Alignment means living authentically, with actions, values, and intuition working in harmony.

2. Misalignment often stems from ignoring intuition, seeking external validation, or losing touch with core values.

3. Practical steps like clarifying values, listening to intuition, and mindful decision-making foster alignment.

4. Overcoming challenges like external pressures or fear of change requires courage, boundaries, and trust in yourself.

5. Aligned living leads to clarity, ease, fulfillment, and a deeper connection to universe knowledge.

Reflection Questions

1. What are your top five core values, and how well do your current actions align with them?

2. Can you recall a decision where you ignored your intuition? What was the outcome, and what did you learn?

3. How might setting daily intentions help you live more in alignment with your purpose?

4. What small, manageable changes could you make to align your work, relationships, or habits with your values?

5. Reflect on a recent moment of alignment. What made it feel so natural, and how can you create more moments like that?

CHAPTER 14
THE ONGOING JOURNEY OF UNIVERSE KNOWLEDGE

THINKING VS THOUGHT

The journey of accessing and living with universe knowledge isn't a one-time event—it's a lifelong process. Like a river that carves its path over time, your connection to universal wisdom deepens as you learn, grow, and adapt. Each step forward offers new insights, each challenge shapes your resilience, and each action aligns you more closely with your higher purpose.

This final chapter reflects on how to sustain and nurture your connection to universe knowledge, embrace the ever-evolving nature of life, and walk your path with trust, curiosity, and courage.

CHAPTER FOURTEEN: THE ONGOING JOURNEY OF UNIVERSE KNOWLEDGE

Understanding the Journey

Unlike fixed goals or destinations, the journey of universe knowledge is fluid and dynamic. As your experiences expand, so does your understanding, allowing you to:

- Approach challenges with greater clarity and wisdom.

- Deepen your intuition and trust in the flow of life.

- Continuously refine your actions to align with your purpose.

Key Principles of the Journey:

1. **There's No Finish Line:** Growth is ongoing, and every stage of life brings new opportunities for learning.

2. **Flexibility is Essential:** As circumstances change, so must your mindset and strategies.

3. **Reflection Fuels Progress:** Regularly pausing to assess your path ensures continued alignment with universe knowledge.

Example: *A person who begins their journey seeking professional success might later shift their focus to building relationships, community, or personal fulfillment. This evolution reflects the natural ebb and flow of life's priorities.*

Embracing Change as Part of Growth

Change can be unsettling, but it's also a powerful catalyst for growth. By viewing change as a teacher, you open yourself to new possibilities and insights.

Steps to Embrace Change:
1. **Release Resistance:** Accept that change is inevitable and necessary for progress.

2. **Seek the Lesson:** Ask yourself, "What can I learn from this situation?"

3. **Adapt with Intention:** Align your actions with the new circumstances while staying true to your core values.

Example: *A career setback might feel like failure at first but could lead to a more fulfilling path by prompting you to reassess your priorities and explore new opportunities.*

Sustaining Your Connection to Universe Knowledge

1. Daily Practices
Consistency is key to maintaining your connection to universe knowledge. Incorporate habits that foster mindfulness, intuition, and alignment into your routine.

Suggested Practices:
- **Morning Intention-Setting:** Begin each day by reflecting on your goals and purpose.

- **Mindfulness Breaks:** Pause throughout the day to ground yourself and tune into your intuition.

- **Evening Reflection:** End your day by journaling lessons learned or moments of alignment.

2. Lifelong Learning
Stay curious and open to new ideas, experiences, and perspectives. The more you explore, the more universe knowledge reveals itself.

Ways to Continue Learning:
- Read books across diverse disciplines.

- Attend workshops, lectures, or spiritual gatherings.

- Seek wisdom from mentors, peers, and even unexpected sources.

3. Build a Supportive Environment
Surround yourself with people, spaces, and resources that align with your values and encourage growth.

Example: *Joining a community of like-minded individuals—whether it's a creative group, spiritual circle, or professional network—can inspire and motivate you to stay on your path.*

Navigating Setbacks with Grace

Even on the path of alignment, setbacks are inevitable. Whether it's an unexpected challenge, a moment of doubt, or a period of stagnation, these experiences are opportunities to deepen your resilience and trust.

How to Navigate Setbacks:
1. **Recenter Yourself:** Use mindfulness or meditation to ground your thoughts and emotions.

2. **Reevaluate Your Path:** Reflect on whether adjustments are needed to realign with your purpose.

3. **Seek Support:** Don't hesitate to lean on trusted friends, mentors, or resources for guidance.

Example: *An artist facing creative block might take a step back, explore new mediums or sources of inspiration, and reignite their passion through experimentation.*

Celebrating Your Progress

Reflection and gratitude are essential for acknowledging how far you've come and reinforcing your connection to universe knowledge.

Reflection Exercise:
- List three moments from the past year when you felt deeply aligned with your purpose.

- Identify the lessons or growth these moments brought you.

- Express gratitude for the journey and the opportunities ahead.

CHAPTER FOURTEEN: THE ONGOING JOURNEY OF UNIVERSE KNOWLEDGE

The Legacy of Universe Knowledge

As you continue your journey, your actions, insights, and alignment will naturally create a ripple effect, inspiring others to explore their own connection to universe knowledge.

Examples of Impact:
- Sharing your story can encourage others to trust their intuition and pursue their passions.

- Small, aligned actions—like kindness, mentorship, or advocacy—can create lasting change in your community.

Key Insight: *Living authentically isn't just a gift to yourself—it's a contribution to the world around you.*

Closing Thoughts

Your journey with universe knowledge is uniquely yours, shaped by your experiences, values, and aspirations. It's a path of discovery, growth, and alignment that offers infinite possibilities. By staying present, trusting the flow, and taking aligned action, you can navigate life with confidence and purpose, knowing that universal wisdom is always within reach.

·················· Key Insights ··················

1. Universe knowledge is an ongoing journey of learning, growth, and alignment, not a destination.

2. Embracing change, setbacks, and evolution deepens your connection to universal wisdom.

3. Daily practices like mindfulness, reflection, and intention-setting sustain your alignment with universe knowledge.

4. Sharing your journey inspires others and amplifies the ripple effect of aligned living.

5. The path of universe knowledge offers clarity, purpose, and fulfillment, no matter where life takes you.

Reflection Questions

1. How has your understanding of universe knowledge evolved throughout your journey?

2. What daily practices or habits could you implement to deepen your connection to universal wisdom?

3. Reflect on a recent setback. What lessons did it offer, and how can you use those lessons moving forward?

4. How might sharing your journey with others inspire or guide them on their own path?

5. What does living in alignment with universe knowledge mean to you, and how will you continue to embody it in your life?

ABOUT THE AUTHOR

Mike Jensen II is a Life Performance Coach with over 12 years of experience helping individuals achieve the greatest performance of their lives and live up to their potential. He holds several certifications in Energy Leadership, Mental Toughness Training, Professional Coaching, and the Science of Happiness. Mike writes a daily short blog on various social media platforms under MBR3 Coaching, which has been updated every day for over eight years without fail. His blog focuses on encouraging others to think outside the box, recognize the abundance around them, and choose a different way to live.

When he's not writing or blogging, Mike is coaching clients all over the world. In his personal time, he enjoys spending time with his amazing wife, family, and especially his grandchildren. Although Mike has lived all over the United States, he always returns to Ottawa, Kansas, a small town he loves for its smallness, slowness, and quietness.

Mike has dedicated his life to serving others, helping them find sustainable happiness and live up to their potential. He believes that everyone has a purpose and unlimited potential.

ABOUT THE PUBLISHER

Dear Reader,

As you hold this remarkable book in your hands, we want to express our heartfelt gratitude for becoming a part of the Live Life Happy Community of readers. Your curiosity and thirst for knowledge fuel our passion for publishing meaningful non-fiction works.

At Live Life Happy Publishing, our mission is rooted in bringing forth literature that not only entertains but uplifts, supports, and nourishes the soul. We firmly believe that books have the power to transform lives, to ignite passions, and to spread joy far and wide.

Behind every word, every chapter, lies the dedication of our authors who pour their hearts and souls into their craft. Their ultimate aim? To touch your life in profound ways, to inspire, and to leave an indelible mark on your journey.

Your role in this journey is invaluable; by sharing your thoughts through reviews, spreading the word to others, or reaching out to the authors themselves, you become an integral part of sparking transformation in countless lives, igniting a ripple effect of joy and enlightenment.

And if, perchance, you or someone you know has dreams of writing, of sharing a message, or of unleashing a powerful story unto the world, know that Live Life Happy Publishing stands ready to guide you. Our doors are open, our ears attuned, and our hearts eager to hear your message.

So, dear reader, let us, continue to spread the power of literature, one page at a time. Reach out, share, and most importantly, never underestimate the power of your message to touch lives.

With warmest regards,

LiveLifeHappyPublishing.com

P.S. Remember, books change lives. Whose life will you touch with yours?

www.ingramcontent.com/pod-product-compliance
Lightning Source LLC
LaVergne TN
LVHW051246080426
835513LV00016B/1766